The Anatomy of The
PERFECT COMPANY

The Checklist for What an Excellent Company Should Look Like, and How an Excellent Company Should Behave.

Author Warren Thompson, Jr.

Preface

There are many available books in the public realm that you may read, or that you may have read, as a company execution, manager, owner, supervisor, or business reader, that will go to great detail, with theories, backed-up with charts, statistics, anecdotes, and examples, indicating what you should be doing to make your organization, or business, a great business, or enterprise, versus the mediocre company that you are currently running today, but this is not one of those books.

To tell the truth, most business people, and business readers, already have plenty of real life experiences, and examples, that they are witnessing in their day-to-day work experience. This book just reminds you that it isn't brain surgery. It's common-sense. There are standards, that most people already know, to judge whether their company, or organization, are already doing things well, or not.

I would suggest that we already know, as customers,

and users of products and services, when we are receiving great service, or are using a product that meets, or exceeds, our expectations. This book reinforces those common-sense standards, and, perhaps, gives you a checklist of standards of what the excellent company do, or should being doing. It suggest to you what those qualitative differences are between the great companies, versus the all-so-ran, or mediocre companies. If you need help in judging who is excellent, who's not, then I believe you already know, but may not have created a checklist of the common-sense qualitative standards, which I believe all companies, or organization, should be judged by.

If you are an owner, manager, executive, supervisor, or business reader, then this book will assist you in focusing on those areas of your organization you may need to improve toward getting on the path of becoming a better, if not excellent company. There are many companies, that you already know, and see, in your business experience, and as a consumer, that meet most of these standards. Many of the "excellent" companies are ones that are probably receiving great success, accolades, and adoration from their customers, competitors, and the communities they belong to and serve, versus those companies that are not currently receiving the same kind of attention reserved for those "excellent" companies. I strongly suggest you use this book to assist you on the path toward reviewing the functioning of your organization, or company, to help you in improving your operations with the goal of becoming an improving, more successful organization.

Acknowledgements

I want to acknowledge my personal thanks to the following close friends and relative for their brilliant suggests and encouraging words while I was undertaking this project, "Perfect Company". Without their positive influence, and intelligent suggestions, this work may not have been as well written and creative.

Thank you Mom, Mary Louise Thompson, for your positive encouragement and great eye for detail. In addition, your cooking is still the best in the world, as evidenced by the May fans you have every day requesting a plate of your great dinners. One day, I hope you allow me to be your co-writer on a cook book detailing some of your delicious recipes.

Thank you Richard Scott III, aka "Blue", for your friendship and professionalism demeanor. Your sense of professionalism and entrepreneurial spirit was extremely encouraging. One day, I hope we do a project together that is worthy of your talents.

I also would like to give a special thanks to Sheila Jean Dennison for being such an inspiration, and encouraging to persevere, in the completion of this project.

Thank to all of you, and all those not mentioned, for your positive encouragement, which any creative venture needs to grow, survive and become reality.

Contents

Chapter One

The Right Way of Doing Business

In the fall of 1977, Nelson Lee Stevens, moved to Pittsburgh, Pennsylvania for a job as a personal lines claims adjuster for the Paul Revere Insurance Company. Nelson actually worked in their suburban Monroeville, PA office.

Nelson worked with a number of hardworking and interesting people; most notable was a man by the name of Lawrence Sheffield. He worked as personal lines, homeowners and automobile, damage appraiser. His duties were primarily to appraise the insurance related casualty damages to homes and automobiles for Paul Revere Insurance Company policyholders. Lawrence would appraise the insurance related damages, write-up a detailed estimated cost of repair, and negotiate with the contractors or auto garages doing the repairs. He seemed competent at his job, as well as friendly and intelligent individual. We became friends, and often went to lunch together.

One Monday morning Lawrence came to work driving a new car, which he purchased over the weekend. It was a mid-sized auto, a Volkswagen Jetta. It was not an expensive automobile, but nice, and brand new. Over lunch that day, Nelson asked his friend, and fellow employee, Lawrence Sheffield, all the pertinent and usual questions about his new car. What did it cost? What was the gas mileage? Etc.

When Nelson asked how much he paid for the car and what Lawrence paid for the down payment, and what he would pay in monthly payments, Lawrence responded by telling Nelson that he had paid cash for the automobile. When Lawrence told Nelson this he was shocked!

Nelson thought he knew, roughly, what Lawrence's salary was, which was certainly less then his salary. Nelson was a college graduate, from the Ohio State University, with a bachelorate degree in business administration, and Lawrence was a high school graduate. Nelson was impressed! Confused, but Nelson did not want to pry into Lawrence's personal affairs, and ask where Lawrence got the money to afford to pay cash for a new automobile.

A few months later, in the late Summer of 1979, my friend, Larry Sheffield, and fellow employee, was going on a deer hunting vacation, which in western Pennsylvania is a very popular tradition for many hunters born and raised in the western Pennsylvania area. In any case, Lawrence had requested six weeks of vacation from his employer, the Paul Revere Insurance Company, and was granted the full six weeks, three weeks without pay. Lawrence only had accrued three weeks, as a five plus year employee with the company, and was taking an additional three weeks without pay.

Upon learning this, Nelson knew that he had to pry, at the risk of offending this fellow employee and friend, and ask Larry, at their next shared lunch outing, how he could afford to buy a new car with cash in full, and afford to take six weeks vacation, three without pay, on a salary as a personal lines insurance damage appraiser. Larry told me over lunch that day, in a somewhat secretive way, that he would invite me to his home for dinner sometime and we could talk further at this, and he would explain to me how he could afford these things, which impressively got my attention.

A few weeks later, Larry did invite Nelson to his home, where Lawrence grilled some stakes, and they had a few beers. Lawrence was so gracious and cool in his demeanor, and Nelson wondered when he was going to tell him about his great fortune. As you can imagine, Nelson's thoughts and imagination made him guess that, perhaps, Lawrence had inherited monies from a relative who may had died, or he had won a lottery prize, etc.

Eventually, Lawrence shared with Nelson, after we finished our steaks, and after a couple of beers, what his big secret was. In fact, it was no secret at all. Larry Sheffield told Nelson that since he as a young boy, with a paper route, delivering newspapers, that he had learned to become a life-long saver. Lawrence would save part of his money that he earned weekly form his earnings from his paper route, and over time, this became a habit he would continue all of his life through to adulthood. Lawrence saved as a teenager from after school, part-time jobs, and he continued his saving habit as an adult up to this date.

Lawrence did not share with me how much money he had saved to date, in his bank account, but he did share with Nelson that, as an adult in his late 30's, he was now in a position to pay cash for all of his basic needs, from buying a car, clothing, vacations, etc. The only liability Lawrence said that he had was the mortgage on his home. Lawrence had a couple of credit cards, but whatever he charged, during a given month, he would pay-off in full when the bill would come due. Lawrence was, essentially, debt-free, except for his home mortgage obligation.

At the end of the evening, Nelson was even more impressed with his friend, Larry Sheffield, to learn that this simple habit, of learning to be a life long saver would make all the difference in the world, from being a person who lived paycheck-to-check, to learning to live a life of relative financial security. Larry's secret, or the lesson Nelson took away from my dinner, and meeting, was that having a consistent life long habit of being a saver was "The Smartest Personal Financial Decision Ever". You don't have to be a financial genius, or get inherited money from some rich relative, or win the lottery, all you have to do is learn a better way of managing your personal finance. You just had to learn to be a life long saver.

Larry Sheffield a life of relative personal financial freedom, somewhat free of financial worries, and was well on his way, barring any catastrophic financial event, to having a financially secure life, and eventual retirement.

However, even if he ran into the unavoidable financial setback, from some unpredictable event, his life long ingrained habit of being a faithful saver, would guide him to financial security, again, and he would handle that unpredictable catastrophic event better then he would have, had he not had his personal savings to help him through the event.

Nelson was now a firm believer that beyond learning to investing in equities, or real estate, or even being a successful entrepreneur, or successful businessperson, learning to be a saver, and being responsible with your personal financial is one of "the smartest personal financial decisions ever" that a person can make.

Chapter Two

Excellent Products and Services

Nelson Lee Stevens never looked at things the same after that dinner and conversation with his friend, Lawrence Sheffield. He saw the wisdom of how the simple, but intelligent habit of being a saver could make in his life. He set out to change his ways, and the he managed his personal financial affairs. In other words, he became a born-again person committed to becoming a life-long saver.

At first, Nelson found it extremely difficult to again any traction in his efforts to save money on a regular basis. It seemed like every time he accumulated any monies of note, there was an emergency or reason to withdraw find from his meager savings account. It seemed like everything went wrong to conspire against his new decision to emulate his friend, Lawrence Sheffield, and become a committed saver.

The normal things that he was use to paying for, like auto repairs, shopping sprees for the newest clothing or consumer product, expensive lunches, going out with friends on the weekends, and other luxuries, seem to be events that were causing him not to be able to gain any traction in his efforts to save money.

Everything seem to be working against him until he learned to say "no", not to his friends would might call to ask him out on a Friday, or Saturday, evening to have fun. He had to learn to say "no" to himself. He realized that he, and his current lifestyle, and spend thrift way, were his own worst enemy. All he had to do was look in the mirror for the reason he could not get his financial house in order. He realized that he had very little discipline when it came to restraining his spending. He was always acting like a kid in a candy store, never saying no to anything. He was a person who lived to satisfy all of his immediate imposes. I guess you could say that he lived for instant gratification.

Once he realized his problem, which was a lack of financial discipline, he was able to focus on his goal of being more of a saver, and getting his financial house in order. He had to learn to strengthen his inner strength, and discipline, and chose what was most important to him. He worked to develop the inner strength, and discipline, to change his behavior, and habits, that were counter productive to creating smarter personal financial habits.

Nelson learned to continue to do many of the things he always enjoyed doing, such as dinner with friends, or shopping on the weekends to buy new clothing or consumer products, etc., but he learned to plan better and to set a budget for his expenses, including budgeting for savings. Once he learned to budget, and be more discipline about his spending and saving, he was on his way to realizing "the smartest personal financial decision ever" for himself.

Once he started saving on a regular basis, it wasn't a matter of regularly putting aside savings every month, from his pay check from his job as a claims adjuster, it was a matter of setting a goal of how much to save. That is to say, "how much should I save?" What's my savings goal?

Nelson's initial goal was just to save a $1,000. Once he reached that goal, which took him several months, he raised his goal to $2,000. After reaching that goal, he raised his goal to 10% of his annual salary, with was, at that time, only $35,000. Once he reached that goal, he set a longer term goal of six months salary, with at the time was $17,500, but was a moving target due to his receiving annual raises at his job, as a claims adjuster. Once he reached that targeted goal, he raised his goal by $5,000 increments every time he would reach his goals going forward. Nelson became a very successful saver.

Over time, Nelson was transformed, and so were his person finances. Over time, as his savings account grew, he managed to reduces his discretionary liabilities, such as his credit card balances, auto loan, and insurance

payments to lower levels. Nelson found that not only did he become a successful saver, but an excellent negotiator when shopping on all his necessities, and luxuries, from his clothing to vacation travel. Nelson was truly a changed man.

Nelson was well on his way to emulating his friend, Lawrence Sheffield, and be coming a person who manages their personal finances in a very intelligent fashion. He found that he could afford many nice things that many of his friends could not afford. He started to feel he could do many things he once only imaged, or dreamt, about, such as international travel, buy the home of his dreams, and planning for a comfortable retirement.

Nelson was always thankful for meeting his friend,

Lawrence Sheffield, and for the wisdom of becoming a saver that Larry shared with him. Nelson felt that he wanted to share this story and lesson with anyone who would listen. He would often repeat what he called "The Lawrence Sheffield Story". and how this lesson changed his life. He still believes that is it "the smartest personal financial decision ever" that he made in his life.

Chapter Three

Employee Relations

I guess you might say "The Secret is really no secret at all"., and you would be right! Yet, there are so many people that grow-up either never being taught this secret, or lesson, or never understand the power of one basic lesson which would set them up, literally, for life on a path toward a better financial future.

Unfortunately, far to many people fall into the trap of living paycheck-to-paycheck, spending every dollar, and living beyond their means, spending more then they earn on a consistent and regular basis. In fact, far to many people fall into the credit trap, or treadmill, that keeps them indebted, practically, from cradle to grave, living and working to pay the minimum month payment, on their maxed-out credit limits cards, and other credit accounts.

This kind of poor personal financial money

management can set a person up for a lifestyle of chasing the next new purchase while at the same time living on the edge of going from one financial emergency to the next. It can only be an existence of living beyond ones needs, always working to pay off yesterdays indulgences, rather then planning intelligently for your future needs, wants, and future dreams.

This can be psychologically an existence of going from the high of the most recent must-have-purchase, to the depression of worrying how you're going to pay for it all when your next monthly bill comes due. It has been suggested that living a life of such anxieties can cause increased stress, ill health, and poor decision making, due to the constant pressure of the emotional stress of the constant crushing debt load over time.

I sincerely believe that learning, and practicing, this lesson can, not only, help you manage your personal finances better, but it can improve your psychological, and physical, health. I implore you, if you haven't already learned, and are practicing, this lesson, to put it into practice starting immediately, today!

Chapter Four

Community Relations

When I had dinner that evening, with Larry Sheffield, what Larry was trying to conveying to me was "The Wisdom of Saving". Whether this lesson, of being a life long saver was taught to him by his parents, from his childhood with them teaching him explicitly, or implicitly from their living example, or if he learned from his own life experiences, Larry was sharing with me the wisdom of his lifetime of experience of being a life long, consistent saver.

Far to many people grow-up believing that you have to be born into wealth, or be a super star in their profession, and be promoted to the highest levels of the company they work for, or win the lottery, or win at the gambling casino tables in Las Vegas, Nevada, or Macau, China, but the truth is that you have a greater change, and easier path, to financial success simply by exercising "The Wisdom of Saving".

Your chances of greater financial success, or even becoming wealthy, are mathematically greater just by becoming a consistent life long saver, and learning to be responsible with the management of your personal finances. You don't have to be a financial genius, investing in the stock market, or extremely successful as an entrepreneur, or phenomenally lucky, and pick the Mega-Million-Dollar lottery ticket drawing, though there's nothing wrong with being smart, well-educated, hard working, or lucky, but your chances are far greater, whether you are male, female, black, white, poor or middle class, of being financially successful by simply being a constant, life long save, and exercising "The Wisdom of Saving".

Chapter Five

Lead or Follow the Trend

Gratification should never be instant! If you are an impulsive buyer of cars, houses, clothes, shoes, plane tickets, etc., unless you've got a bank account like Willard "Mitt" Romney, you may be an emotional, or impulsive, shopper, which is rarely good for your personal financial management, and it makes it hard to be a good saver of money when you buy for emotional, non-budgeted reasons.

You may feel great while you are in the moment, buying that new car, suit, shoes, or plane ticket to Hawaii, but, if it's an unwise purchase, at this point in time, based on your current financial situation, then, you may not only be making a bad financial decision, you may, additionally, feel bad later, about your decision to buy that new car, suit, or whatever, once the excitement of having that new car in your driveway fades.

If you are using shopping as emotional therapy to combat your depression, over the break-up with your girl-friend, or boy friend, or being turn down for that well deserved promotion, etc., you will soon find out that your shopping spree is only a temporary fix, and may even serve to contribute to make you feel worst later, as you struggle to pay for your latest shopping therapy session.

In fact, one of the greatest antidotes for an emotional funk, and to exit from the emotional, financial roller coaster, is the good feeling of having a significant bank saving account, and significantly more stable financial lifestyle. Far to many people don't realize the emotional difference between living on the financial brink of a paycheck-to-paycheck existence, versus the emotional stability, and confidence, that comes from managing your personal finances in a more responsible way, by incorporating regular, consistence saving into their personal financial life.

I implore you to learn the important lesson in this book, and learn to be more discipline personal financial manager, and to resist the impulse of using shopping, "Instant Gratification", as a therapy to cure your occasional emotional bad day, or rough emotional episode. "The Smartest Personal Financial Decision Ever!" that you may ever learn is to become a live long saver. It may be the best medicine, and therapy, for your emotional depression.

Closing Comments

To reiterate, I tried to do my best not to overstate, or exaggerate, about the importance of this lesson, I finally decided that there are very few lessons in life that I believe will make a more profound difference then this lesson, or in making this decision. As I see it, this is one of "the smartest personal financial decisions ever" that a person can make for himself or herself.

That decision is to be a life-long saver of the monies you earn, or acquire. It is my firm belief that how well you manage your personal finances will reflect directly on whether you are in control of your life, or whether financial events, or responsibilities, or other people, will control the decision you make about your life.

This one lesson, or decision, can make the difference between living paycheck to paycheck, and a life of abundance. It can make the difference between poverty and wealth, a life filled with financial stress, or ease.

I strongly suggest you learn and incorporate this lesson into your life, and how you manage your personal financial affairs. If you do, you will be going down a path of greater financial security, financial success, and greater happiness. I implore you to read, learn, and practice this lesson. It, without a doubt, will be "the smartest personal financial decision ever" that you make.

In the telling of "The Lawrence Sheffield Story", I changed the names of the principle of this story, and the names of the insurance company we worked for to de-emphasis the personalities, including myself, and the organization we work for because the lesson is not unique to the personalities, or the organization. In other words, the real importance is the lesson and not the individuals or organizations mentioned.

Thank you for reading -

The Anatomy of The Perfect Company

"THE CHECK LIST FOR WHAT AN
EXCELLENT COMPANY SHOULD
LOOK LIKE, AND HOW AN
EXCELLENT COMPANY SHOULD
BEHAVE."

Author Warren Thompson, Jr.

Other books I have written are -

THE HAMBURGER STORY OF INVESING

Author Warren Thompson, Jr.

"THE SMARTEST PERSONAL FINANCIAL DECISION EVER!"

FEATURING "THE LAWRENCE SHEFFIELD STORY"

Author Warren Thompson, Jr.

OLD SCHOOL LESSONS THAT STILL GET A PASSING GRADE

Author Warren Thompson, Jr.

IS THIS THE BOOK YOU'VE BEEN LOOKING FOR?LD SCHOOL LESSONS THAT STILL GET A PASSING GRADE

35 Answers for Uncommon Questions

Author Warren Thompson, Jr.

www.ingramcontent.com/pod-product-compliance
Lightning Source LLC
Chambersburg PA
CBHW030045230526
45472CB00005B/1677